Sports Stars

SUGAR RAY LEONARD

The Baby-faced Boxer

By Bert Rosenthal

CHILDRENS PRESS, CHICAGO

Cover photograph: Ron Fine
Inside photographs courtesy of the following: Harry Dunn, pages 6, 8,
11, 13, 22, and 38; Ron Fine, pages 19, 27, 29, 32, 36, and 40;
Jack M. Douthitt, page 25; Andrew D. Bernstein, page 34; Steve Schwartz, page 17.

Library of Congress Cataloging in Publication Data

Rosenthal, Bert.
  Sugar Ray Leonard, the baby-faced boxer.

  (Sports stars)
  Summary: A brief biography of "America's
Sweetheart," the welter weight champion boxer.
    1. Leonard, Sugar Ray, 1956-   —Juvenile
literature. 2. Boxers (Sports)—United States
—Biography—Juvenile literature. [1. Leonard,
Sugar Ray, 1956-   . 2. Boxers (Sports)
3. Afro-Americans—Biography] I. Title.
II. Series.
GV1132.L42R67   796.8'3'0924 [B] [92]   82-4472
ISBN 0-516-04326-9   AACR2

        6 7 8 9 10 11 12 R 90 89 88 87

Sports Stars

SUGAR RAY LEONARD

The Baby-faced Boxer

Boxing is a rough sport. The idea is to hit your opponent as hard as you can with your fists.

Sugar Ray Leonard does not look like a fighter. He does not appear to have a mean streak in his body. He is always smiling and happy. He could pass for a choir boy. He has a baby face. It's a face that has few marks on it, although it has taken a lot of punches.

Yet, Sugar Ray is one of the best fighters in the world. Some people even rate him among the best boxers in history.

Boxing is a rough sport. The idea is to hit your opponent as hard as you can with your fists.

"He has as much natural ability as any boxer who ever laced on gloves. And he's dedicated to becoming the best," said Angelo Dundee, Sugar Ray's manager. "He's already one on the best I ever saw."

Despite his success, Sugar Ray admits he still is scared every time he steps into the ring.

"I'm scared," he admitted. "I'm not afraid of the person I'm fighting. It's just the natural fear. It's just a matter of waiting for your time, when the people come and say, 'Fifteen minutes till fight time,' 'Ten minutes,' 'Five minutes.' They worry me. And all the people coming to the dressing room saying, 'Good luck, man.'"

The fear never has left Sugar Ray even though he has been fighting for nearly half his life.

"I never get used to it," he said. "But there are fighters who will not admit that they're scared."

Being scared, however, does not mean Sugar Ray thinks he will lose.

"Whenever I step into the ring, I feel dominant and confident," he said.

He has every right to feel confident. He is an outstanding fighter. No one in boxing has faster hands than Sugar Ray. He can deliver dazzling combinations quickly, accurately, and with power. His foot speed is also excellent. His big punch is a left hook. But he also can hurt an opponent with a right-hand blow. He doesn't often knock out his rivals with one punch, but with a series of punches.

He doesn't often lose, either. His professional career began in 1977. He has lost only once. That defeat was on a close decision to Roberto Duran on June 20, 1980. It was a 15-round fight for Sugar Ray's World Boxing Council welterweight (147-pound) title.

Sugar Ray got back the title five months later. He stopped Duran in eight rounds.

The following year Leonard added another title — the World Boxing Association junior middleweight (154-pound) crown. He won that by knocking out Ayub Kalule in nine rounds. Then he won worldwide recognition as welterweight chamption by stopping WBA titleholder Thomas "Hit Man" Hearns in 14 rounds.

Sugar Ray has been fighting for nearly half his life. But he still is scared every time he steps into the ring.

Sugar Ray won his first title — the WBC welterweight crown — by stopping Wilfred Benitez in the 15th round on November 30, 1979.

Those four fighters — Duran, Kalule, Hearns, and Benitez — had a combined record of 177 victories, only one loss, and one draw decision when they fought Leonard. Sugar Ray beat them all. Furthermore, Kalule and Hearns never had lost. They never had been knocked down. Sugar Ray knocked them both down. Then he went on to hand each one his first defeat.

All this by a man who never intended to be a professional fighter.

After winning the gold medal in the light welterweight division (141-pound) at the 1976 Olympic Games, Sugar Ray said he planned to give up boxing. He was going to enter the University of Maryland. He wanted to be the first person in his family to go to college.

But both his parents became very sick. Sugar Ray had to support them, plus his girl friend, Juanita, and their son, Ray Jr. He had little choice other than to go to work. Since he had become a hero at the Olympic Games, he turned to boxing. It was a job he did well. He could make money quickly — if he were successful.

Sugar Ray actually had begun fighting when he was 14 years old. Two years later, he won his first amateur title. His record as an amateur was 145 victories and five losses, with 75 knockouts. He won the gold medal at the 1975 Pan American Games.

The next year he became an Olympic champion. He won six fights in 13 days at the Summer Games in Montreal. He stood out from the other fighters because of the red, white, and blue tassles that hung from his shoes and because he taped a picture of Juanita (whom he later married) and Ray Jr. to his sock.

Sugar Ray and Juanita during their wedding ceremony. They and their son
Ray, Jr. live in the countryside in Maryland.

When he turned pro in 1977 it was with great fanfare. Although his first fight was only a six-rounder against Luis Vega, it was billed as the main event. Main events generally are 10, 12, or 15 rounds.

But this fight was on national television. President Carter was extended a personal invitation to attend. Sugar Ray won an easy decision. The next fight was not as easy.

"I nearly got my block knocked off," said Sugar Ray. "Willie Rodriguez, the guy I fought, had a bit more experience."

That fight, which Sugar Ray won after six rounds, made him realize how tough it was to be a professional boxer.

Sugar Ray's trainer, Angelo Dundee, is on the right.

"That's when I said, 'Man, these guys are hitting harder and harder,'" he recalled.

Nevertheless, Sugar Ray remained unbeaten. He was fighting often. He was earning a lot of money. And he was becoming even more popular.

"Then I started meeting guys who were tougher, stronger, and had a lot more experience," said Leonard. "I fought Marcos Geraldo (on May 20, 1979). He was a middleweight (160-pound division). He hit me in the third round and cleaned my clock.

"That made me think again that it's not worth it. But then I came back and won the title (from Benitez) and felt it was okay."

It was okay until he was beaten by Duran. He then told Juanita he never would fight again. She didn't believe him.

"No more, no more. That's it. I'm through," he told her.

Sugar Ray and Juanita went on a two-week vacation in Hawaii. For the first week Sugar Ray never mentioned the Duran fight or what he planned to do in the future.

Getting ready for a workout.

"But I knew it was on his mind," she said.

Finally, he admitted to her, "I can't stop fighting."

"I was expecting it," she said. "There was no way he was going to quit at 25. It's his career. But that's not really it. Fighting is in his blood. He's going forward, not backward. All I can do is stand behind him."

Financially, Leonard did not have to fight again. He already had earned millions of dollars — and invested it wisely. He could retire to the new home he had built in Mitchellsville, Maryland. He also had received lots of money for doing things outside the ring.

He had made television commercials, including one for 7-Up with Ray, Jr. He had appeared on TV as a commentator during boxing matches, and on many talk shows. He also had joined a local TV station in Washington, D.C. as a sports reporter. He covered boxing and other sports.

And he hoped to eventually host his own talk show.

It would have been easy to walk away from boxing. Juanita and Ray, Jr. would have been very happy. Neither one likes to see him in the ring. They are very proud, of course, when he wins. But there is always the chance he will get hurt — and that is what they fear.

Marion Barry, the mayor of the District of Columbia, and Sugar Ray.

So Sugar Ray, who said, "I love my sport," decided to fight Duran again. And he fought one of the best fights of his life. Duran surprisingly quit in the eighth round.

Sugar Ray had gotten even for the only loss of his pro career. And he had embarrassed the man who was called "Hands of Stone," in respect to his powerful fists.

In 1981 Sugar Ray added to his marvelous record. He knocked out Larry Bonds in 10 rounds. He beat Kalule and he beat Hearns. For those three magnificent performances, he was named Sportsman of the Year by *Sports Illustrated* magazine.

The award is one of many that have been won by Sugar Ray. Ray, Jr. calls him one of America's "Greatest People," because "he is a good boxer" and "a good father" and "a good husband." Also, because, "most of all he is my best friend."

The love between Ray and Ray Jr. is genuine. So is the love between Ray and Juanita.

Success has not spoiled Sugar Ray. Unlike many fighters, he has taken care of his money. He has provided well for his family. From a family that was virtually without money only a few years ago, the Leonards have become millionaires.

Sugar Ray has only lost once, and that was a close decision.

It is a position that Sugar Ray values very highly. When he was growing up as the youngest of a family of seven children in Wilmington, North Carolina, he had little money.

"We were dirt poor," he remembered. "The kids wore hand-me-downs and we weren't fat."

He was named after his mother's favorite singer, Ray Charles.

"I went from singing to swinging," Sugar Ray says with a smile.

When Sugar Ray was born, the family moved from Wilmington to Washington, D.C. because one of his brothers said there was money to be made there. When he was 10, the family moved to nearby Palmer Park, Maryland.

Ray's grandfather, Bidge, had been a fighter back in Carolina. And his father, Cicero, also was considered a good fighter in his younger days. But he didn't tell his son.

"I never knew my father was a fighter until I was already a fighter," said Sugar Ray. "I was about 14 or 15 and we went back to North Carolina. I heard all my father's buddies talking about how good he used to be."

Cicero never taught his son to fight.

"Ray was fighting six months before I saw him," said Cicero. "I never encouraged him. Boxing is tough. He just had it in him.

"He was 12 or 13 and he said, 'Dad, I can box.' So he got me to come see him."

Sugar Ray's big punch is a left hook. But he can hurt with his right hand, too.

Cicero was amazed at what he saw.

"I saw him and said, 'That's me. My God, that's me again.'"

Sugar Ray had learned to box in the Palmer Park Recreation Center. He had taken up boxing after turning down other sports or getting hurt in them.

In basketball he was not big enough or strong enough. He quit wrestling in junior high school after suffering a severe arm injury. He tried track and ran cross country. But muscle injuries in his legs forced him to quit. He also gave up gymnastics after nearly breaking his neck attempting a back flip. And he tried football, but he couldn't afford a uniform.

The same thing was true when he wanted to join the Boy Scouts — he couldn't afford a uniform.

Now, he can afford almost anything. His home cost $750,000. It has a swimming pool, a pool house, and courts for basketball and tennis.

Having a lot of money also can be a burden, explained Sugar Ray. He said the more money he has, the more people he doesn't really know want to be his friends. He also receives many requests to make big donations.

"I want to help," he said, "but it is not easy to know what is worthwhile. And you need more to support yourself."

Working with youngsters is something Sugar Ray likes. It seems the kids like it too.

While Sugar Ray guards his money carefully, he gives freely of his time. He is very active in charity groups and community work. He enjoys working with youngsters. He says that if he were not a fighter, he probably would be a youth director.

Ever since he started, Sugar Ray has been the glamour boy of boxing. He took over where former world heavyweight champion Muhammad Ali left off—at least in the United States. While Ray has yet to achieve Ali's fame throughout the world, Sugar Ray has certainly matched it in this country. He is easily the most recognized fighter in the game today.

The fans love Sugar Ray. They love to come to his public workouts. He gives them copies of his picture.

"He is America's sweetheart," said a boxing promoter in Arizona. "He's another Shirley Temple. Everybody falls in love with him."

They fall in love with him because of his engaging personality. They love his big, wide smile, his cute wink, his poise, his perfect way of speaking, his friendliness and the neat, clean manner in which he dresses. They love to come to his public workouts, because he gives away free copies of his picture. On each picture is his autograph and the word, "Peace." For his title fight against Bruce Finch on February 15, 1982, he ordered $1,200 worth of hand towels with the letters SRL on them, which he planned to give out to training camp visitors. (He got that idea

from the late rock-and-roll singer, Elvis Presley, who used to give handkerchiefs to his admiring fans.)

Kids love him because he works with them. He talks to them about dedication, sacrifice, going to school, and working hard.

Sugar Ray knows all about working hard.

"I've worked my way up from the bottom, step by step, to a point so many fighters only hear about," he said proudly.

How long will he remain there?

"My ambition is to retire financially independent," he said. "I don't want to be just a good fighter. I want to be something special.

Sugar Ray intended to fight more fights. He once said, "I could stop in a couple of years, in a couple of fights. After that, I'd like to do some TV commentary, maybe some acting, and be a part-time counselor for school kids.

"I don't want to fight too long," he added. "Boxing can take a heavy physical toll." Then, May 8, 1982, when Sugar Ray was training for a title fight against Roger Stafford, he was hurt. Ray complained of an eye injury.

The next day he had an operation for a detached retina. The retina is like the film in a camera. Images focus on the retina before they are sent to the brain.

A week later, Sugar Ray left the hospital. His eye was better. But Sugar Ray thought a long time, then retired from boxing.

Everyone thought he would just work for television as a boxing announcer after that. But Ray kept watching boxing. He wished he could still fight.

One day he changed his mind. He said he would fight. A match was set up. But when the fight came, Sugar Ray was not ready. He boxed poorly, and just beat a very average boxer, Kevin Howard. Ray announced his retirement again. That was in 1984. Everyone believed Sugar Ray was through.

But, Sugar Ray couldn't stop thinking about Marvelous Marvin Hagler. Hagler was the middleweight champion of the world. They said Hagler could not be beaten. Ray would have had a chance to fight Hagler if he had not hurt his eye. Sugar Ray could not stop thinking that he could beat Hagler.

In 1986 he shocked the world. He said he would fight Hagler. Even Hagler could not believe it. More than 100 days after Ray challenged him, Hagler accepted the fight. Yet, no one thought Sugar Ray could win. He had not had a good fight in five years!

"I wasn't mentally ready fo fight Howard," Sugar Ray explained.

But Marvin Hagler was a great champion. He had held the title for nearly 7 years, through 12 title defenses. He was one of the finest middleweight champions of all time. Could Sugar Ray have a chance?

Sugar Ray worked very hard. He got ready. He believed in himself. He set up the fight for only 12 rounds. He knew he would get tired before Hagler got tired. He planned to be clever and smarter than Hagler.

It was a long fight. At the end of 12 rounds both fighters were still fighting. The judges had to decide who had won. One judge said Hagler. A second judge said Leonard. That left it up to the third judge. The ring announcer looked at the score. Then he announced, "The winner, by a split decision, and *new* middleweight champion of the world, *Sugar Ray Leonard*!"

Sugar Ray had done it. He had won. He kissed his wife, Juanita, and his sons, Ray Jr., and Jarrel (who is named after Jor-el, the father of Superman). "Everything I did worked," he said. "I went against history and now they have to rewrite the history books. People said I lost the zip, but my hands are just as fast as they were when I was 20 years old."

Sugar Ray's record was now 34-1. He had earned more than $52 million as a boxer. He lived in a seven-bedroom mansion that looks like a castle. He had four very expensive cars. He had everything, because he believed in himself. And he worked hard to get what he wanted.

Now he was the champion again.

CHRONOLOGY

1956—Ray Charles Leonard is born on May 17.

1970—Sugar Ray begins boxing.

1972—He wins his first amateur title.

1975—Sugar Ray wins a boxing gold medal at the Pan American Games in Mexico City.

1976—He wins the light welterweight boxing gold medal at the Summer Olympic Games in Montreal.

1977—Sugar Ray makes his professional debut and wins a six-round decision over Luis Vega.

1979—On November 30, Sugar Ray wins the World Boxing Council welterweight title, stopping Wilfred Benitez in the 15th round.

1980—Sugar Ray marries his childhood sweetheart of nine years, Juanita Wilkinson, on January 18 at Landover, Maryland.

—Leonard defends his welterweight title for the first time, knocking out Dave "Boy" Green in the fourth round on March 31.

—On June 20, he loses the title on a 15-round decision to Roberto Duran.

—Sugar Ray regains the title on November 25, stopping Duran in the eight round.

1981—Sugar Ray captures the World Boxing Association junior middleweight title by knocking out Ayub Kalule in the ninth round on June 25.

—He gains worldwide recognition as welterweight champion on September 16 by stopping WBA champion Thomas Hearns in the 14th round.

1982—In January, Sugar Ray is named Sportsman of the Year for 1981 by *Sports Illustrated*.

—Sugar Ray undergoes an eye operation in May, putting his boxing career in jeopardy.

—In November Sugar Ray retires from boxing.

1984—Sugar Ray had a comeback fight May 11 and again retired—this time, he said, for good.

—On June 14 Sugar Ray's wife Juanita gave birth to their second son, Jarrel Guilio Leonard.

1987—On April 6 Sugar Ray becomes the New World Middleweight Champion defeating Marvin Hagler, by a 2-1 decision in favor of Sugar Ray.

ABOUT THE AUTHOR

Bert Rosenthal has worked for the Associated Press for nearly 25 years. He has covered or written about virtually every sport. But his first love is professional basketball. Mr. Rosenthal is the author of Sports Stars books on Larry Bird, Darryl Dawkins, and Marques Johnson.

He was AP's pro basketball editor from 1973 until 1976. From 1974 until early 1980, he was the secretary-treasurer of the Professional Basketball Writers' Association of America. He has been a co-author on two books—*Pro Basketball Superstars of 1974* and *Pro Basketball Superstars of 1975*. For the past five years Mr. Rosenthal has been editor of HOOP Magazine, an official publication of the National Basketball Association.

At present, he is the AP's track and field editor, and a frequent contributor to many basketball, football, and baseball magazines.